TABLE OF CONTENTS

CHAPTER 1

PLAY BALL!

The **pitcher** winds up. He throws. The ball speeds toward home plate.

HISTORY OF SPORTS

THE HISTORY OF BASEBALL

by Brendan Flynn

pogo

Ideas for Parents and Teachers

Pogo Books let children practice reading informational text while introducing them to nonfiction features such as headings, labels, sidebars, maps, and diagrams, as well as a table of contents, glossary, and index.

Carefully leveled text with a strong photo match offers early fluent readers the support they need to succeed.

Before Reading

- "Walk" through the book and point out the various nonfiction features. Ask the student what purpose each feature serves.
- Look at the glossary together. Read and discuss the words.

Read the Book

- Have the child read the book independently.
- Invite him or her to list questions that arise from reading.

After Reading

- Discuss the child's questions. Talk about how he or she might find answers to those questions.
- Prompt the child to think more. Ask: What did you find most surprising about the history of baseball? Why?

Pogo Books are published by Jump!
5357 Penn Avenue South
Minneapolis, MN 55419
www.jumplibrary.com

Library of Congress Cataloging-in-Publication Data

Names: Flynn, Brendan, 1968- author.
Title: The history of baseball / By Brendan Flynn.
Description: Minneapolis, MN: Jump!, Inc., [2025]
Series: History of sports | Includes index.
Audience: Ages 7-10
Identifiers: LCCN 2023054696 (print)
LCCN 2023054697 (ebook)
ISBN 9798892130714 (hardcover)
ISBN 9798892130721 (paperback)
ISBN 9798892130738 (ebook)
Subjects: LCSH: Baseball–History–Juvenile literature. Baseball players–Juvenile literature. | World Series (Baseball)–History–Juvenile literature.
Classification: LCC GV867.5 .F59145 2025 (print)
LCC GV867.5 (ebook)
DDC 796.357–dc23/eng/20231229
LC record available at https://lccn.loc.gov/2023054696
LC ebook record available at https://lccn.loc.gov/2023054697

Editor: Alyssa Sorenson
Designer: Molly Ballanger

Photo Credits: Library of Congress, cover (left), 14-15, 16-17tl; Mike Flippo/Shutterstock, cover (right); jonathansloane/iStock, 1, 3, 23; Jamie Lamor Thompson/Shutterstock, 4; Seregal/Dreamstime, 5; Frank Romeo/Shutterstock, 6-7; clu/iStock, 8 (left); Aeromass/Shutterstock, 8 (right); Suzanne Tucker/Shutterstock, 9; Piemags/PL Photography Limited/SuperStock, 10-11; Robert F. Cranston, Frank Livia, Bill Klein, Harry Warnecke/Circa Images/Glasshouse Images/SuperStock, 12; Keystone View Company/Archive Photos/Getty, 12-13; General Photographic Agency/Getty, 16-17tr; Bruce Bennett/Getty, 16-17bl; Diamond Images/Getty, 16-17br; 4x6/iStock, 18; Glenn Nagel/Dreamstime, 19; Rob Tringali/MLB Photos/Getty, 20-21.

Printed in the United States of America at Corporate Graphics in North Mankato, Minnesota.

The **batter** swings. He hits the ball. It goes over the fence. It's a home run! Baseball is a popular sport. The best athletes play in Major League Baseball (MLB).

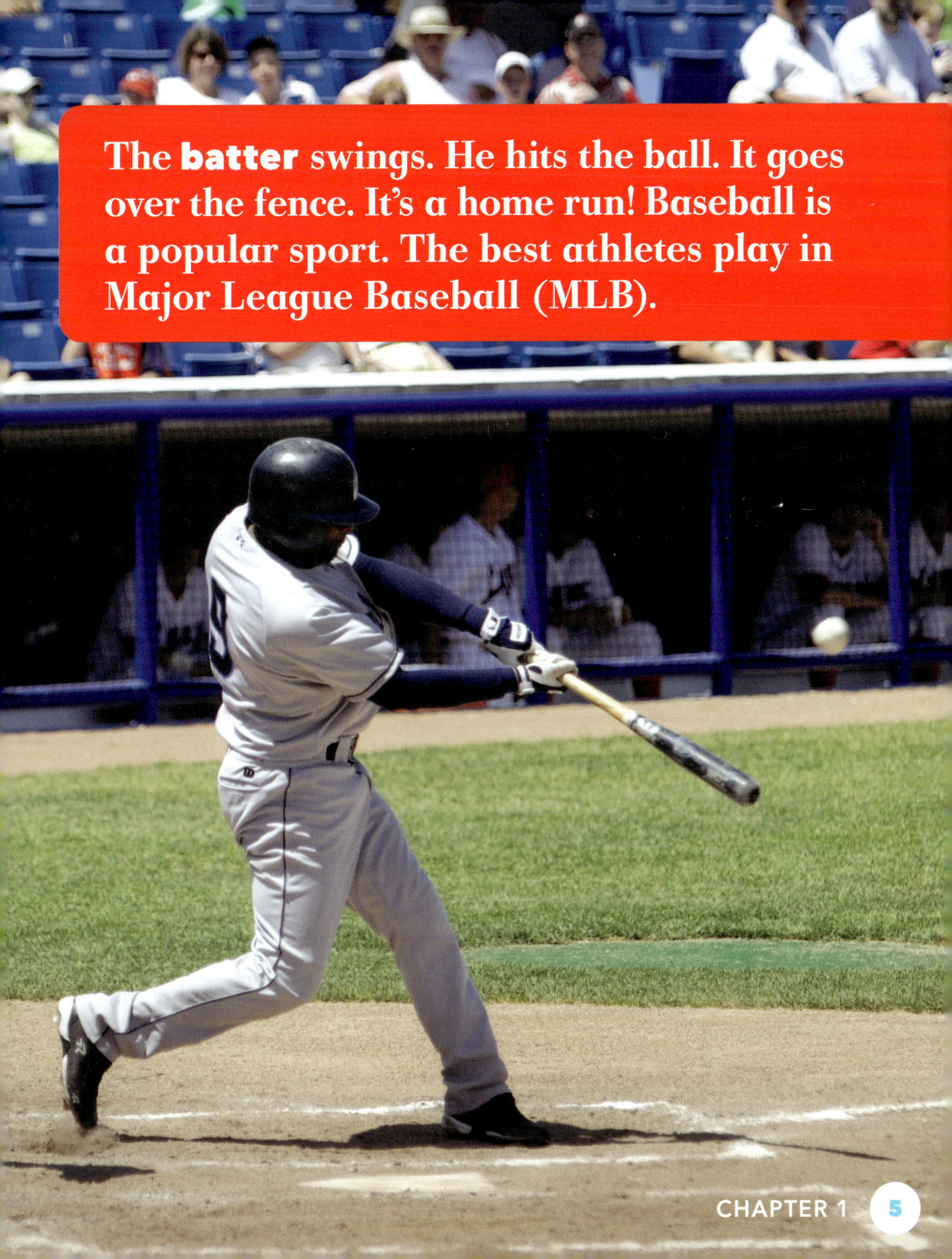

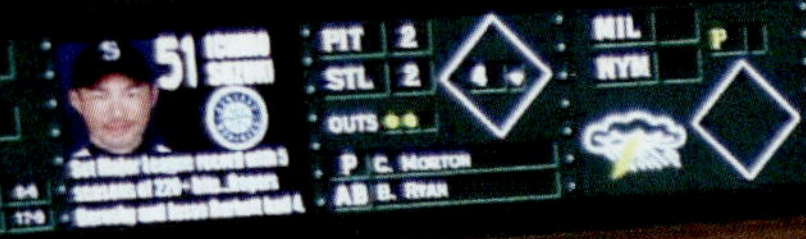

Baseball is played on a diamond. Batters are on the **offense**. They want to hit the ball. If they do, they try to run around all four bases. They want to get back to home plate. Why? They want to score a run. The **defense** tries to catch and throw the ball to get them out. The team with the most runs wins.

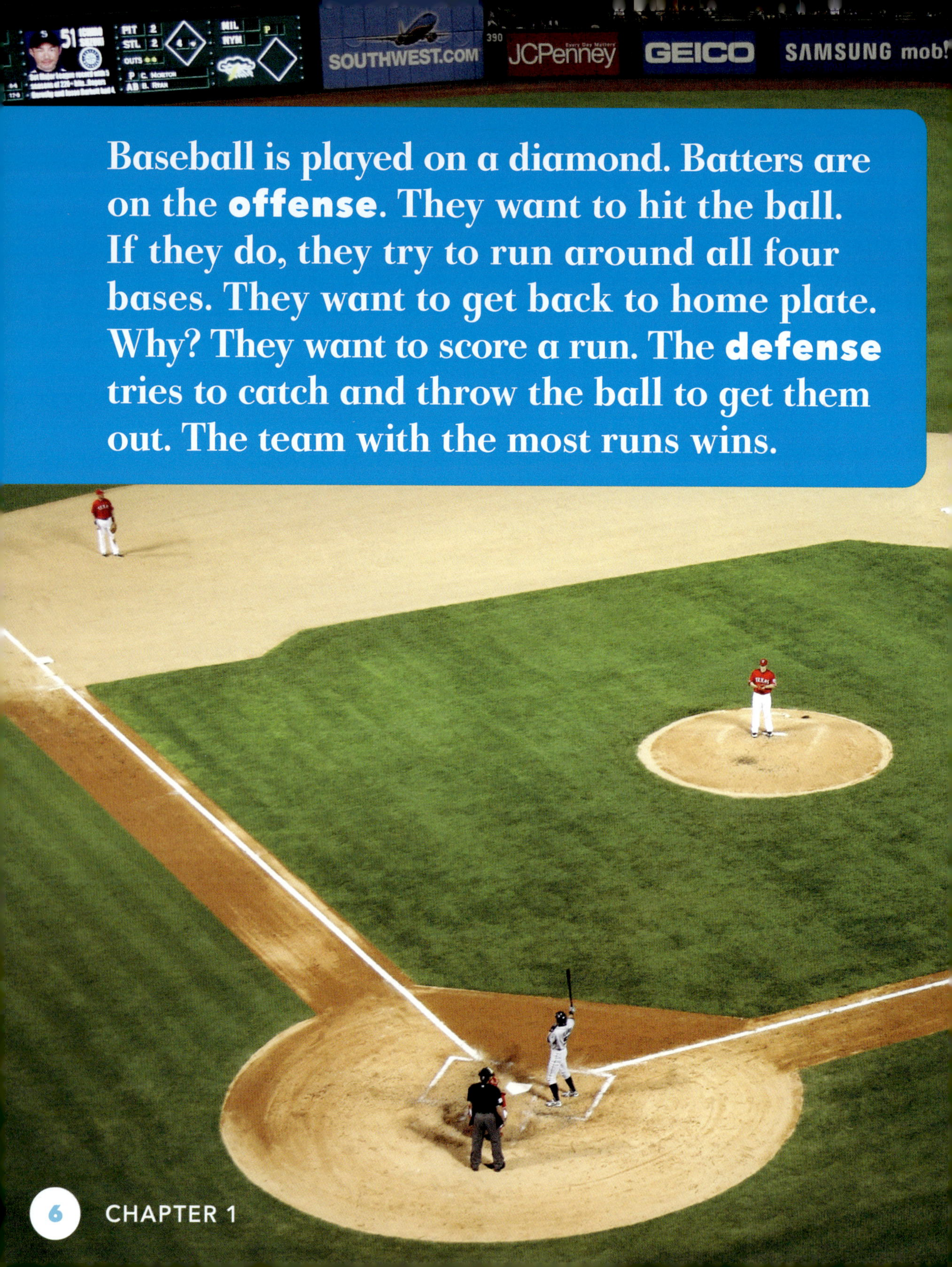

TAKE A LOOK!

Where do players stand on the baseball diamond? Take a look!

SECOND BASE

THIRD BASE

FIRST BASE

HOME PLATE

PITCHER'S MOUND

1. pitcher
2. catcher
3. first baseman
4. second baseman
5. shortstop
6. third baseman
7. left fielder
8. center fielder
9. right fielder
10. batter

CHAPTER 2

BASEBALL'S HISTORY

When baseball first started, players did not wear gloves. Now, every player in the field wears one.

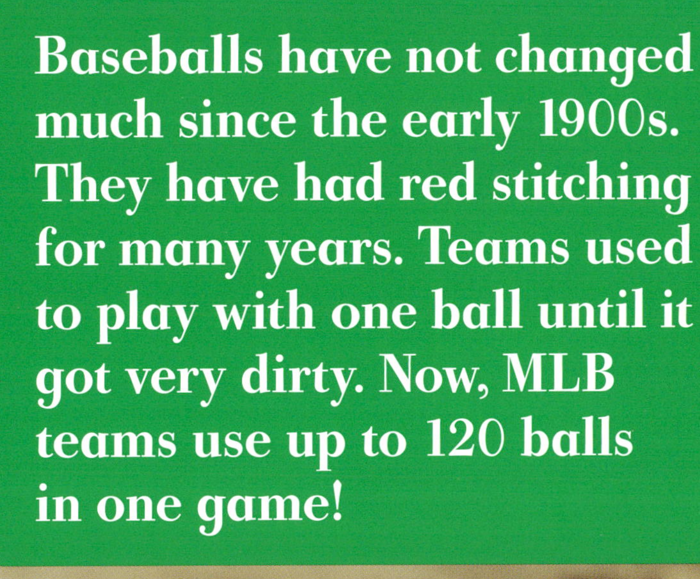

Baseballs have not changed much since the early 1900s. They have had red stitching for many years. Teams used to play with one ball until it got very dirty. Now, MLB teams use up to 120 balls in one game!

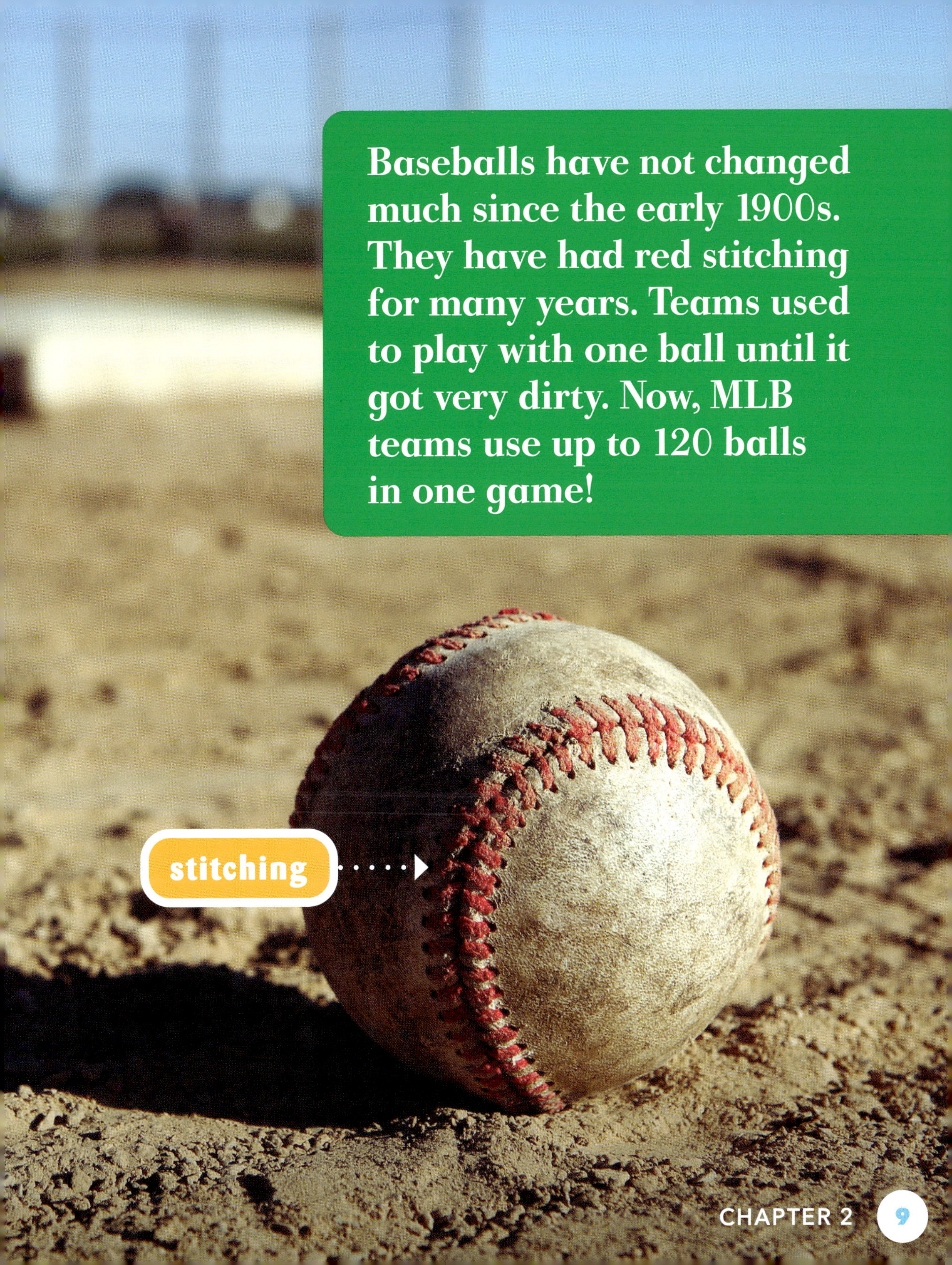

stitching

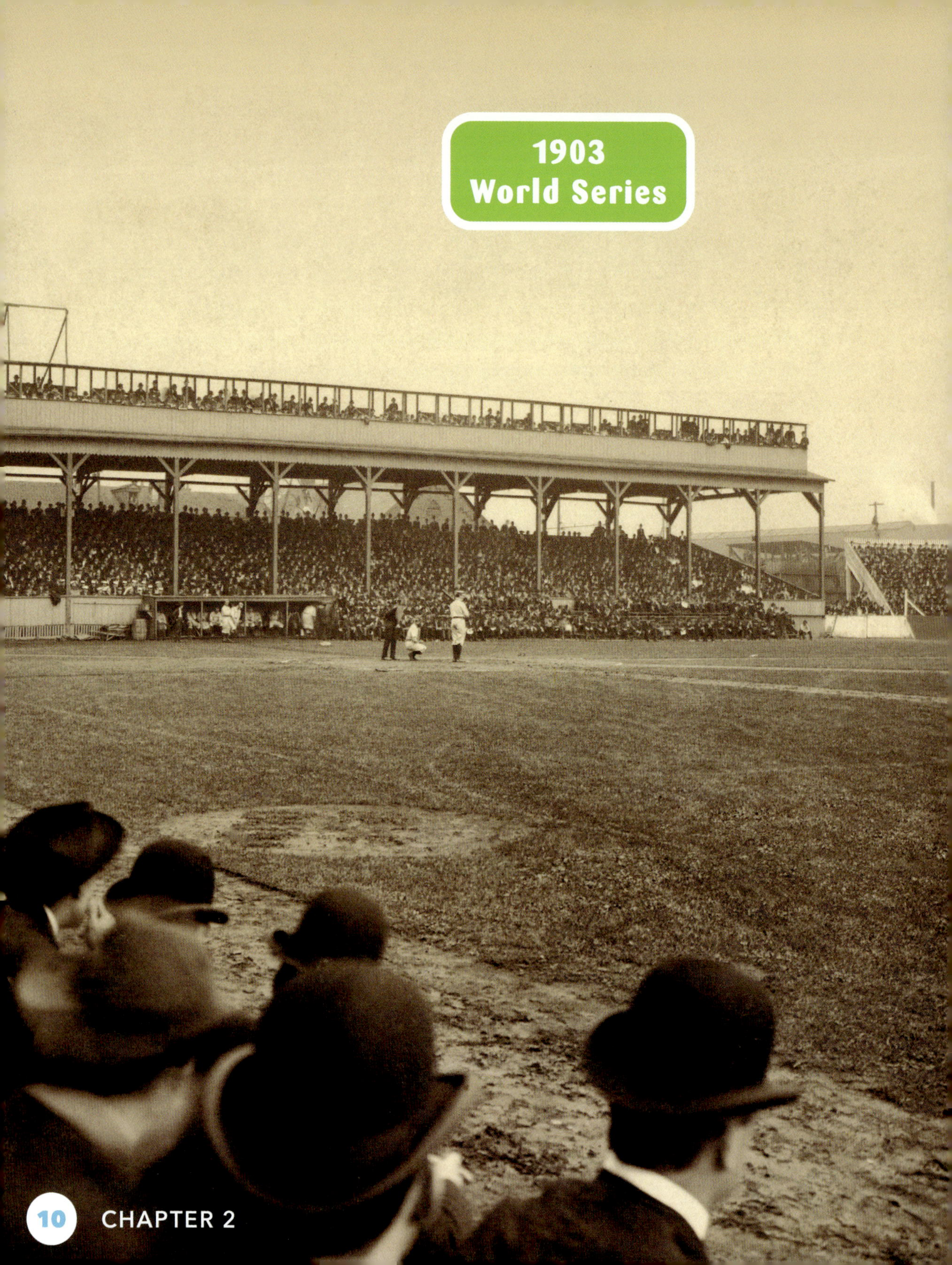

1903 World Series

Two leagues make up MLB today. The National League (NL) started in 1876. The American League (AL) followed in 1901.

The best NL and AL teams play in the World Series. There are seven games. Whoever wins the most is the MLB champion. The first World Series was in 1903. The Boston Americans played the Pittsburgh Pirates. Boston won!

DID YOU KNOW?

Which team has won the most World Series? It is the New York Yankees. As of 2023, they had won 27!

In the early days, Black players were not allowed in MLB. The Negro Leagues gave them a chance to show their skills.

Jackie Robinson was a Black baseball player. In 1947, the Brooklyn Dodgers asked him to play on their MLB team. Robinson was a star. Soon, other MLB teams let Black players join.

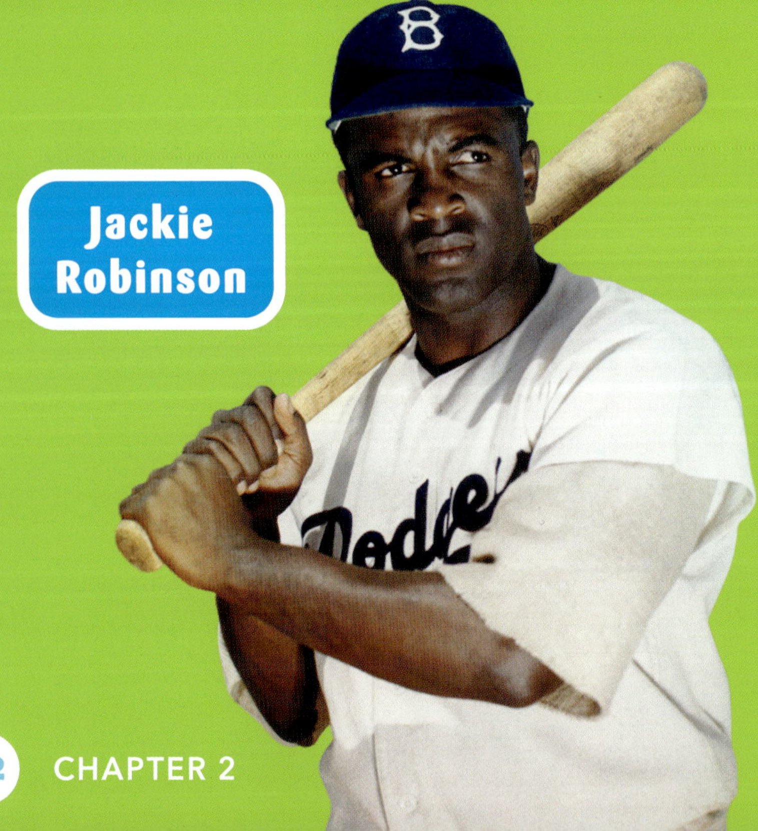

Jackie Robinson

NEW YORK
CUBANS
14

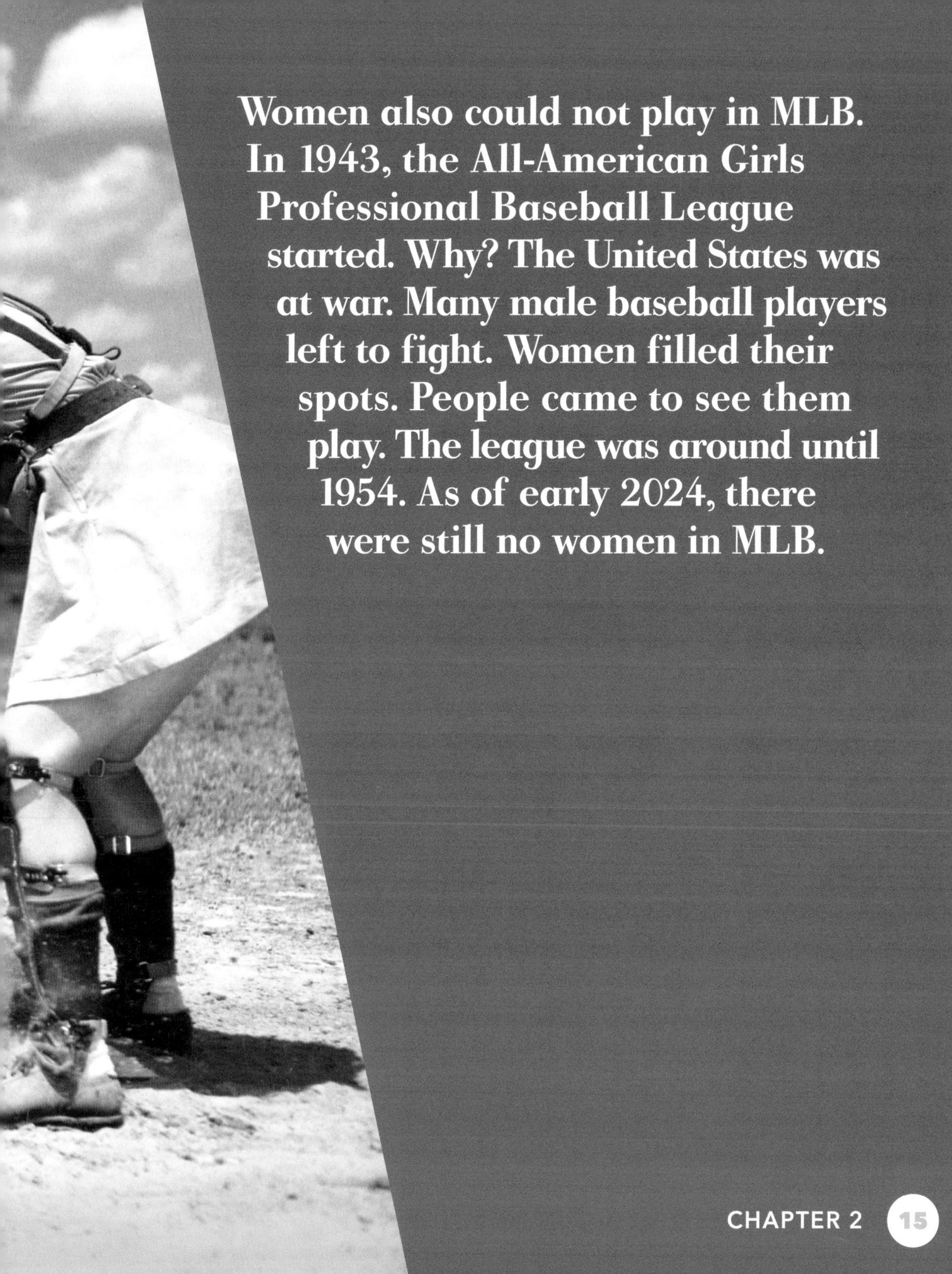

Women also could not play in MLB. In 1943, the All-American Girls Professional Baseball League started. Why? The United States was at war. Many male baseball players left to fight. Women filled their spots. People came to see them play. The league was around until 1954. As of early 2024, there were still no women in MLB.

There have been many great MLB players. Cy Young won more games than any other pitcher. Babe Ruth was on the Yankees. He helped them win in the 1920s. Satchel Paige was the best pitcher in the Negro Leagues. Boston's Ted Williams may have been the best hitter ever.

WHAT DO YOU THINK?

Think about a great athlete. What makes them great?

Cy Young

Babe Ruth

Satchel Paige

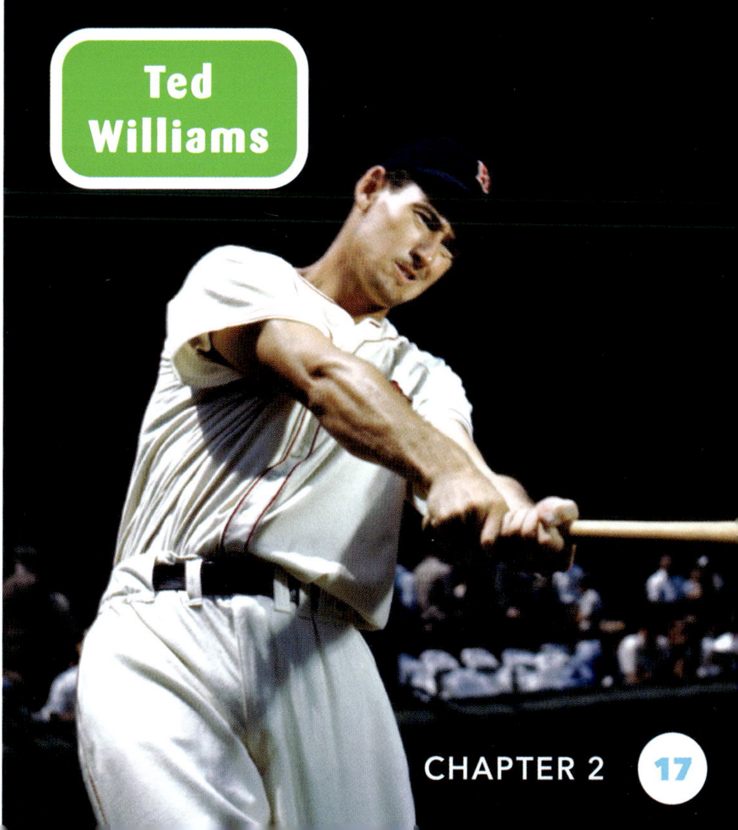

Ted Williams

CHAPTER 3

BASEBALL TODAY

Baseball looks a lot like it did 100 years ago. The basic rules are the same. Even the uniforms have not changed much. Players still wear a cap and jersey. They wear pants, socks, and **cleats**.

MLB games are played in big **stadiums**. These did not always have lights. Games were played during the day. Now, most are played at night. There are big, electronic scoreboards. Why? They show **highlights**. People see **statistics**.

Today, **fans** watch pitchers throw fastballs at 100 miles (161 kilometers) per hour. They cheer when players like Mike Trout hit home runs. MLB players today follow in the footsteps of the all-time greats. Baseball's **traditions** are one reason fans still enjoy the game.

WHAT DO YOU THINK?

In 2023, MLB added a pitch clock. Pitchers have either 15 or 20 seconds to throw the ball. This helps the game move faster. Why do you think some people want a fast-paced game?